TO

_____

FROM

_____

FIRST CUP
DEVOTIONS

FOR
TEACHERS

Scripture quotations are taken from:

The Holy Bible, King James Version

The Holy Bible, New International Version (NIV) Copyright © 1973, 1978, 1984, by International Bible Society. Used by permission of Zondervan Publishing House. All rights reserved.

The Holy Bible, New King James Version (NKJV) Copyright © 1982 by Thomas Nelson, Inc. Used by permission.

The New American Standard Bible®, (NASB) Copyright © 1960, 1962, 1963, 1968, 1971, 1972, 1973, 1975, 1977, 1995 by The Lockman Foundation. Used by permission.

Holy Bible, New Living Translation, (NLT)copyright © 1996. Used by permission of Tyndale House Publishers, Inc., Wheaton, Illinois 60189. All rights reserved.

The Message (MSG)- This edition issued by contractual arrangement with NavPress, a division of The Navigators, U.S.A. Originally published by NavPress in English as THE MESSAGE: The Bible in Contemporary Language copyright 2002-2003 by Eugene Peterson. All rights reserved.

New Century Version® (NCV) Copyright © 1987, 1988, 1991 by Word Publishing, a division of Thomas Nelson, Inc. All rights reserved. Used by permission.

The Holman Christian Standard Bible™ (HCSB) Copyright © 1999, 2000, 2001 by Holman Bible Publishers. Used by permission.

Cover Design by Kim Russell / Wahoo Designs
Page Layout by Bart Dawson

ISBN 1-58334-275-3

Printed in the United States of America

FIRST CUP
DEVOTIONS

FOR
TEACHERS

TABLE OF CONTENTS

INTRODUCTION: FIRST THINGS FIRST

DON'T BE IN ANY RUSH TO BECOME A
TEACHER, MY FRIENDS. TEACHING IS HIGHLY
RESPONSIBLE WORK. TEACHERS ARE HELD TO
THE STRICTEST STANDARDS.

JAMES 3:1 MSG

Henry Adams correctly observed, "A teacher affects eternity; he can never tell where his influence stops." And, those words have never been more true than they are today. We live in a difficult, fast-paced, temptation-filled world; more than ever, our young people need the direction and the leadership provided by teachers who place God first in their lives.

Does God come first in your life *and* your day? Do you awaken early enough to enjoy that first cup of hot coffee while studying your Bible and spending at least a few quiet moments with your Creator? Or are you one of those people who sleeps until the last possible minute, leaving no time to invest in matters of the heart and soul? Hopefully, you make a habit of spending precious moments each morning with your Father in heaven. When you do, He will fill your heart, He will direct your thoughts, and He will guide your steps.

This book contains devotional readings that are intended to set the tone for the rest of your day. The text is divided into 30 chapters, one for each day of the month. Each chapter contains Bible verses, quotations, brief essays, and prayers, all of which can help you focus your thoughts on the countless blessings and opportunities that God has placed before you.

During the next 30 days, please try this experiment: Read one chapter each morning with your first cup of coffee. If you're already committed to a daily worship time, this book will enrich that experience. If you are not, the simple act of giving God a few minutes each morning will change the tone and direction of your life.

Your daily devotional time can be habit-forming, and should be. The first few minutes of each day are invaluable. Treat them that way, and offer them to God.

IT ALL STARTS WITH GOD

YOU SHALL HAVE NO OTHER GODS BEFORE ME.

EXODUS 20:3 NKJV

How do you begin your day? Do you start your morning with a hot beverage and a sincere chat with God? Well, whether you prefer coffee, tea, hot chocolate, or none of the above, you most certainly should acquire the habit to giving God a few minutes of your time at the start of each day.

In the book of Exodus, God warns that we should place no other gods before Him. Yet all too often, we place our Lord in second, third, or fourth place as we allow the distractions of everyday living to hijack our days and our lives.

The words are as familiar as they are true: "First things first." But sometimes, in the busy world in which we live, placing first things first can be difficult indeed. Why? Because so many people are expecting so many things from us! We have families to care for, students to teach, administrators to please, and bills to pay. What's a teacher to do? The answer to that question is straightforward: we must make God our first priority.

This morning and every morning hereafter, start your day with a time of prayer and consultation with the Giver of all things good. Prioritize your day according to God's commandments; seek His will first, and trust His wisdom. Then, you can face the day with the assurance that the same God who created our universe out of nothingness can help you place first things first in your own life.

«« «« »» »

Be half a Christian, and you will have just enough religion to make you miserable.

C. H. SPURGEON

God calls us to be committed to Him,
to be committed to making a difference,
and to be committed to reconciliation.

BILL HYBELS

God wants to teach us that when we commit
our lives to Him, He gives us that wonderful teacher,
the Holy Spirit.

GLORIA GAITHER

In order to be rightly oriented to God and His work,
you need a God-centered life.

HENRY BLACKABY AND CLAUDE KING

MORE FROM GOD'S WORD

Don't look for shortcuts to God. The market is flooded with surefire, easygoing formulas for a successful life that can be practiced in your spare time. Don't fall for that stuff, even though crowds of people do. The way to life—to God!— is vigorous and requires total attention.

MATTHEW 7:13-14 MSG

TODAY, I WILL THINK ABOUT . . .

Ways that I can glorify God by placing Him first in my life.

A PRAYER TO START MY DAY

Dear Lord, make me a person of unwavering commitment to You, to my family, and to my students. Guide me away from the temptations and distractions of this world, so that I might honor You with my thoughts, my actions, and my prayers. ««Amen

THE JOYS OF TEACHING

YOU WILL TEACH ME HOW TO LIVE
A HOLY LIFE. BEING WITH YOU WILL
FILL ME WITH JOY; AT YOUR RIGHT HAND
I WILL FIND PLEASURE FOREVER.

PSALM 16:11 NCV

Teaching can and should be a joyful experience. Of course, as every veteran teacher knows, some days are more challenging than others. But even on the most difficult days, we can find pockets of satisfaction, islands of peace, and moments of joy.

Psalm 100 reminds us that, as believers, we have every reason to celebrate: "Shout for joy to the LORD, all the earth. Worship the LORD with gladness" (vv. 1-2 NIV). Yet sometimes, amid the inevitable hustle and bustle of life here on earth, we can forfeit—albeit temporarily—the joy that God intends for our lives. C. H. Spurgeon, the renowned 19th-century English clergyman, advised, "Rejoicing is clearly a spiritual command. To ignore it, I need to remind you, is disobedience." As Christians, we are called by our Creator to live abundantly, prayerfully, and joyfully. To do otherwise is to squander His spiritual gifts.

If, today, your heart is heavy, open the door of your soul to the Father and to His Son. Christ offers you His peace and His joy. Accept it and share it freely, just as Christ has freely shared His joy with you.

I find teaching extraordinarily satisfying.

BARBARA JORDAN

Our sense of joy, satisfaction, and fulfillment
in life increases, no matter what the circumstances,
if we are in the center of God's will.

BILLY GRAHAM

Joy is a by-product not of happy circumstances,
education, or talent, but of a healthy relationship
with God and a determination to love Him
no matter what.

BARBARA JOHNSON

According to Jesus, it is God's will that
His children be filled with the joy of life.

CATHERINE MARSHALL

Joy has nothing to do with circumstances.
Joy is a choice. It is a matter of attitude
that stems from one's confidence in God.

CHARLES SWINDOLL

MORE FROM GOD'S WORD

Let the hearts of those who seek the Lord rejoice.
Look to the Lord and his strength; seek his face always.

1 CHRONICLES 16:10-11 NIV

I've told you these things for a purpose:
that my joy might be your joy,
and your joy wholly mature.

JOHN 15:11 MSG

TODAY, I WILL THINK ABOUT . . .

The opportunities, the joys,
and the responsibilities of being a teacher.

A PRAYER TO START MY DAY

Lord, make me a joyous Christian. Because of
my salvation through Your Son, I have every reason
to celebrate—let my joy be evident in every aspect
of life, including my life inside the classroom.
Today, let my words and deeds be a testimony
to Christ's love and to His grace. ««Amen

WHERE WISDOM BEGINS

FOR THE LORD GIVES WISDOM;
FROM HIS MOUTH COME KNOWLEDGE AND
UNDERSTANDING.

PROVERBS 2:6 NKJV

D o you seek wisdom for yourself and for your students? Of course you do. But as a savvy teacher, you know that wisdom can be an elusive commodity in today's world. We live in a society filled with temptations and distractions; it's easy for teachers and students to lose sight of the ultimate wisdom. The ultimate source of wisdom, of course, is the Word of God.

When you begin each day by studying God's Word—and when you live according to His commandments—you will become wise . . . and so, in time, will many of your students. But if you expect a blanket of maturity to settle quietly across the entirety of your classroom, you'll be disappointed. Wisdom is not like a mushroom; it does not spring up overnight. It is, instead, like an oak tree that starts as a tiny acorn, grows into a sapling, and eventually reaches up to the sky, tall and strong.

When you study God's Word and live according to His commandments, you will become a wise teacher . . . and you will be a blessing to your friends, to your family, to your students, and to the world.

Wise people listen to wise instruction,
especially instruction from the Word of God.

WARREN WIERSBE

If we neglect the Bible, we cannot expect to benefit
from the wisdom and direction that result
from knowing God's Word.

VONETTE BRIGHT

Seek wisdom. It's out there.

SHEILA WALSH

Indeed, wisdom and discernment are among
the natural results of a prayer-filled life.

RICHARD FOSTER

The fruit of wisdom is Christlikeness, peace,
humility, and love. And, the root of it is faith
in Christ as the manifested wisdom of God.

J. I. PACKER

MORE FROM GOD'S WORD

Do you want to be counted wise,
to build a reputation for wisdom? Here's what you do:
Live well, live wisely, live humbly.
It's the way you live, not the way you talk, that counts.

JAMES 3:13 MSG

TODAY, I WILL THINK ABOUT . . .

The difference between the world's "wisdom"
and God's true wisdom.

A PRAYER TO START MY DAY

Lord, help me to be a teacher who values both
education and wisdom. Let me instruct my students
by the words that I speak and by the life that I live.
My students deserve no less and neither,
dear Lord, do You. ««Amen

DAY 4

TODAY'S CELEBRATION

THIS IS THE DAY THE LORD HAS MADE;
WE WILL REJOICE AND BE GLAD IN IT.

PSALM 118:24 NKJV

The familiar words of Psalm 118 remind us that today, like every day, is a priceless gift from God. And as teachers, we are doubly blessed: we can celebrate the glory of God's creation, *and* we can celebrate the precious students that He has entrusted to our care.

What do you expect from the day ahead? Are you expecting God to do wonderful things, or are you living beneath a cloud of apprehension and doubt? Do you expect God to use you in unexpected ways, or do you expect another uneventful day to pass with little fanfare? As a thoughtful believer, the answer to these questions should be obvious.

For Christian believers, every new day offers exciting possibilities. God's Word promises that Christ has come to this earth to give us abundant life and eternal salvation. We, in turn, should respond to God's gifts by treasuring each day and using our time here on earth to glorify our Creator and share the Good News of His Son.

Each day is a special gift from God, a treasure to be savored and celebrated. May we—as believers who have so much to celebrate—never fail to praise our Creator by rejoicing in His glorious creation.

All our life is a celebration for us; we are convinced,
in fact, that God is always everywhere.
We sing while we work . . . we pray
while we carry out all life's other occupations.

St. Clement of Alexandria

I know nothing, except what everyone knows—
if there where God dances, I should dance.

W. H. Auden

Celebration is possible only through
the deep realization that life and death are never
found completely separate. Celebration can really
come about only where fear and love, joy and
sorrow, tear and smiles can exist together.

Henri Nouwen

If you can forgive the person you were,
accept the person you are, and believe in
the person you will become, you are headed for joy.
So celebrate your life.

Barbara Johnson

MORE FROM GOD'S WORD

Rejoice in the Lord always. Again I will say, rejoice!

PHILIPPIANS 4:4 NKJV

*At the dedication of the wall of Jerusalem,
the Levites were sought out from where they lived and
were brought to Jerusalem to celebrate joyfully
the dedication with songs of thanksgiving and
with the music of cymbals, harps and lyres.*

NEHEMIAH 12:27 NIV

TODAY, I WILL THINK ABOUT . . .

The need to celebrate God's gifts.

A PRAYER TO START MY DAY

Dear Lord, You have given me so many reasons
to celebrate. Today, let me choose an attitude of
cheerfulness. Let me be a joyful Christian, Lord,
quick to laugh and slow to anger. And, let me share
Your goodness with my family, my friends,
my neighbors, and my students,
this day and every day. ««Amen

THE RIGHT KIND OF EXAMPLE

SET AN EXAMPLE OF GOOD WORKS YOURSELF,
WITH INTEGRITY AND DIGNITY
IN YOUR TEACHING.

TITUS 2:7 HCSB

We teach our students by the words we speak and the lives we lead, but not necessarily in that order. Sometimes, our actions speak so loudly that they drown out our words completely. That's why, as teachers, we must make certain that the lives we lead are in harmony with the lessons we preach.

An important part of God's plan for your life is found in the example that you set for your students. Are you the kind of teacher whose life serves as a memorable model of righteousness and godliness? If so, you are a powerful force for good in your classroom and in your world.

St. Basil, the Bishop of Caesarea, observed, "Teaching a Christian how he ought to live does not call so much for words as for daily example." And that's sound advice because your families and your students are watching . . . and so, for that matter, is God.

Preach the gospel every day; if necessary, use words.

ST. FRANCIS OF ASSISI

A good example is the best sermon.

THOMAS FULLER

Actions speak louder than words;
let your words teach and your actions speak.

ST. ANTHONY OF PADUA

You can preach a better sermon with your life
than with your lips.

OLIVER GOLDSMITH

In our faith we leave footprints to guide others.
A child, a friend, a recent convert.
None should be left to walk the trail alone.

MAX LUCADO

MORE FROM GOD'S WORD

God's Way is not a matter of mere talk;
it's an empowered life.

1 CORINTHIANS 4:20 MSG

Do you want to be counted wise,
to build a reputation for wisdom? Here's what you do:
Live well, live wisely, live humbly.
It's the way you live, not the way you talk, that counts.

JAMES 3:13 MSG

TODAY, I WILL THINK ABOUT . . .

The impact of my example upon family,
friends, and students.

A PRAYER TO START MY DAY

Dear Lord, because I am a teacher, I am an example
to my students. Let me be a worthy example,
Father, so that my words and my deeds
may be a tribute to You. ««Amen

WHOM WILL YOU ENCOURAGE TODAY?

BUT ENCOURAGE EACH OTHER DAILY,
WHILE IT IS STILL CALLED TODAY,
SO THAT NONE OF YOU IS HARDENED
BY SIN'S DECEPTION.

HEBREWS 3:13 HCSB

Life is a team sport, and all of us need occasional pats on the back from our teammates *and* our coaches. As Christians, we are called upon to spread the Good News of Christ, and we are also called to spread a message of encouragement and hope to the world. This world can be a difficult place, and countless students may be troubled by the challenges of everyday life. Our task, as teachers, is to become beacons of encouragement inside the classroom and out.

Each day provides countless opportunities to encourage others and to praise their good works. When we do, we not only spread seeds of joy and happiness, but we also follow the commandments of God's Holy Word.

Today, look for the good in others and celebrate the good that you find. When you do, you'll be a powerful force in the classroom . . . and a worthy servant to your God.

He climbs highest who helps another up.

ZIG ZIGLAR

We have the Lord, but He Himself has recognized
that we need the touch of a human hand.
He Himself came down and lived among us
as a man. We cannot see Him now, but blessed be
the tie that binds human hearts in Christian love.

VANCE HAVNER

The secret of success is to find a need and fill it,
to find a hurt and heal it, to find somebody
with a problem and offer to help solve it.

ROBERT SCHULLER

To the loved, a word of affection is a morsel, but to
the love-starved, a word of affection can be a feast.

MAX LUCADO

Encouraging others means helping people,
looking for the best in them, and trying to bring out
their positive qualities.

JOHN MAXWELL

MORE FROM GOD'S WORD

So encourage each other and give each other strength,
just as you are doing now.

1 THESSALONIANS 5:11 NCV

Let's see how inventive we can be in encouraging love
and helping out, not avoiding worshipping together
as some do but spurring each other on.

HEBREWS 10:24-25 MSG

TODAY, I WILL THINK ABOUT . . .

Creative ways that I can encourage my students.

A PRAYER TO START MY DAY

Dear Father, make me an encouraging teacher.
Just as You have lifted me up, let me also lift up
my students in the spirit of encouragement and
hope. Today, let me help my students find
the strength and the courage to use their gifts
according to Your master plan. ««Amen

THE POWER OF PATIENCE

GOD'S SERVANT MUST NOT BE
ARGUMENTATIVE, BUT A GENTLE LISTENER
AND A TEACHER WHO KEEPS COOL,
WORKING FIRMLY BUT PATIENTLY
WITH THOSE WHO REFUSE TO OBEY.
YOU NEVER KNOW HOW OR WHEN GOD
MIGHT SOBER THEM UP WITH A CHANGE OF
HEART AND A TURNING TO THE TRUTH.

2 TIMOTHY 2:24-25 MSG

Students, even the most dedicated and well-intentioned, are far from perfect. They make mistakes and misbehave; they don't always listen, and they don't always complete their assignments. In an imperfect school filled with imperfect people, a teacher's patience is tested many times each day. But, God's instructions are clear: "be patient, bearing with one another in love" (Ephesians 4:2 NIV). As believers, we must exercise patience, even when doing so is difficult.

Teaching, like every job, has its fair share of frustrations—some great and some small. Sometimes, these frustrations may cause you to reach the boiling point. But here's a word of warning: When you're tempted to lose your temper over the minor inconveniences of the teaching profession, don't give voice to your angry thoughts.

When you make haste to speak angry words, you will inevitably say things that you'll soon regret. Remember that God will help you control your temper if you ask Him to do so. And the time to ask for His help is before your temper gets the best of you—not after.

If only we could be as patient with
other people as God is with us!

JIM GALLERY

Take no action in a fit of anger.
It's putting to sea in a storm.

THOMAS FULLER

Unrighteous anger feeds the ego and produces
the poison of selfishness in the heart.

WARREN WIERSBE

Anger's the anaesthetic of the mind.

C. S. LEWIS

When you get hot under the collar,
make sure your heart is prayer-conditioned.

ANONYMOUS

MORE FROM GOD'S WORD

Patience and encouragement come from God.
And I pray that God will help you all agree
with each other the way Christ Jesus wants.

ROMANS 15:5 NCV

Be still before the LORD and wait patiently for him . . . .

PSALM 37:7 NIV

TODAY, I WILL THINK ABOUT . . .

The need to be a patient, understanding,
compassionate teacher.

A PRAYER TO START MY DAY

Make me a patient teacher, Lord, slow to anger and
quick to forgive. When I am hurried, slow me down.
When I become impatient with others, give me
empathy. Today, let me be a patient servant as I trust
in You, Father, and in Your master plan. ««Amen

STRENGTH FOR THE DAY

THOSE WHO HOPE IN THE LORD
WILL RENEW THEIR STRENGTH.
THEY WILL SOAR ON WINGS LIKE EAGLES;
THEY WILL RUN AND NOT GROW WEARY,
THEY WILL WALK AND NOT BE FAINT.

ISAIAH 40:31 NIV

If you're a teacher with too many obligations and too few hours in which to meet them, you are not alone: yours is a demanding profession. As a dedicated teacher, you may experience moments when you feel overworked, overstressed, and under-appreciated. Thankfully, God stands ready to renew your optimism and your strength if you turn to Him.

When you feel worried or weary, focus your thoughts upon God and upon His love for you. Then, ask Him for the wisdom to prioritize your life and the strength to fulfill your responsibilities. God will give you the energy to do the most important things on today's to-do list . . . if you ask Him. So ask Him.

Because He lives, I can face tomorrow;
because He lives, all fear is gone;
because I know He holds the future,
and life is worth the living just because He lives.

GLORIA GAITHER AND WILLIAM J. GAITHER

Jesus is not a strong man making men and women
who gather around Him weak.
He is the Strong creating the strong.

E. STANLEY JONES

We give strength to our souls as we train ourselves
to speak words of thankfulness and praise.

ANNIE CHAPMAN

There are two things we are called to do:
we are to depend on His strength and be obedient to
His Word. If we can't handle being dependent and
obedient, we will never become the kind of people
who have a heart for God.

STUART BRISCOE

MORE FROM GOD'S WORD

God is our refuge and strength,
a very present help in trouble.

PSALM 46:1 NKJV

I can do all things through Christ who strengthens me.

PHILIPPIANS 4:13 NKJV

TODAY, I WILL THINK ABOUT . . .

The strength that can be mine when I allow Christ
to dwell in the center of my heart.

A PRAYER TO START MY DAY

Dear Lord, I will turn to You for strength.
When my responsibilities seem overwhelming,
I will trust You to give me courage and perspective.
Today and every day, I will look to You
as the ultimate source of my hope, my strength,
my peace, and my salvation. ««Amen

TEACHING DISCIPLINE

GUIDE THE YOUNG MEN TO LIVE
DISCIPLINED LIVES. BUT MOSTLY,
SHOW THEM ALL THIS BY DOING IT YOURSELF,
INCORRUPTIBLE IN YOUR TEACHING,
YOUR WORDS SOLID AND SANE.

TITUS 2:6-8 MSG

As a teacher, you are charged with a thankless task: controlling students who would prefer not to be controlled. Hopefully, your students will learn that disciplined behavior is a prerequisite for success both inside and outside the classroom.

Those who study the Bible are confronted again and again with God's intention that His children (of all ages) lead disciplined lives. God doesn't reward laziness or misbehavior. To the contrary, He expects His own to adopt a disciplined approach to their lives, and He punishes those who disobey His commandments.

Do you teach the importance of discipline? If so, many of your students are learning powerful, life-changing lessons about the rewards of a disciplined lifestyle. And rest assured that your example will speak far more loudly than your lectures. So teach the fine art of responsible behavior through your words and your actions, but not necessarily in that order.

Let us look upon our children;
let us love them and train them as children
of the covenant and children of the promise.
These are the children of God.

ANDREW MURRAY

Better to instruct a child than to collect riches.

ST. HERVE OF BRITTANY

Discipline is training that develops and corrects.

CHARLES STANLEY

Nothing of value is ever acquired without discipline.

GORDAN MacDONALD

The alternative to discipline is disaster.

VANCE HAVNER

MORE FROM GOD'S WORD

If you love learning, you love the discipline that goes with it—how shortsighted to refuse correction!

PROVERBS 12:1 MSG

TODAY, I WILL THINK ABOUT . . .

The need to teach discipline through my words and my actions.

A PRAYER TO START MY DAY

Dear Lord, Your Holy Word tells us that You expect Your children to be diligent and disciplined. You have told us that the fields are ripe and the workers are few. Lead me to Your fields, Lord, and make me a disciplined teacher in the service of Your Son, Christ Jesus. When I am weary, give me strength. When I am discouraged, give me hope. Make me a disciplined, courageous, industrious servant for Your kingdom today and forever. ««Amen

FAITH TO MOVE MOUNTAINS

I TELL YOU THE TRUTH, IF YOU HAVE FAITH
AS SMALL AS A MUSTARD SEED, YOU CAN SAY
TO THIS MOUNTAIN, "MOVE FROM HERE TO
THERE" AND IT WILL MOVE.
NOTHING WILL BE IMPOSSIBLE FOR YOU.

MATTHEW 17:20 NIV

As a dedicated member of the teaching profession, you have mountains to climb and mountains to move. Jesus taught His disciples that if they had faith, they could move mountains. You can too. When you place your faith, your trust, indeed your life in the hands of Christ Jesus, you'll be amazed at the marvelous things He can do.

When a suffering woman sought healing by simply touching the hem of His garment, Jesus turned and said, "Daughter, be of good comfort; thy faith hath made thee whole" (Matthew 9:22 KJV). We, too, can be made whole when we place our faith completely and unwaveringly in the person of Jesus Christ.

Hannah Whitall Smith advised, "Shout the shout of faith. Nothing can withstand the triumphant faith that links itself to omnipotence. For 'this is the victory that overcometh the world.' The secret of all successful living lies in this shout of faith." Christian teachers agree.

So, if your faith is being tested, know that Your Savior is near. If you reach out to Him in faith, He will give you peace, perspective, and hope. If you are content to touch even the smallest fragment of the Master's garment, He will make you whole.

True faith is never found alone;
it is accompanied by expectation.

C. S. LEWIS

Those who make religion consist altogether in
good works overlook the fact that works themselves
are not acceptable to God unless they proceed
from faith. For without faith, it is impossible to
please Him. And those who make religion consist
altogether in faith overlook the fact that true faith
always works by love, and invariably
produces the works of love.

CHARLES FINNEY

The cautious faith that never saws off the limb
on which it is sitting never learns that
unattached limbs may find strange,
unaccountable ways of not falling.

DALLAS WILLARD

Christian faith needs continuous maintenance.

EUGENE PETERSON

MORE FROM GOD'S WORD

So then faith comes by hearing,
and hearing by the word of God.

ROMANS 10:17 NKJV

Thy faith hath made thee whole.

MATTHEW 9:22 KJV

TODAY, I WILL THINK ABOUT . . .

My need to seek God's will and to follow God's Son.

A PRAYER TO START MY DAY

Dear Lord, help me to be a teacher whose faith
is strong and whose heart is pure. Help me to
remember that You are always near and that You can
overcome any challenge. With Your love and
Your power, Lord, I can live courageously and
faithfully today and every day. ««Amen

WITH AN UNDERSTANDING HEART

SO, AS THOSE WHO HAVE BEEN CHOSEN
OF GOD, HOLY AND BELOVED,
PUT ON A HEART OF COMPASSION, KINDNESS,
HUMILITY, GENTLENESS AND PATIENCE.

COLOSSIANS 3:12 NASB

What a blessing it is when our loved ones genuinely seek to understand who we are and what we think. Just as we seek to be understood by others, so, too, should we seek to understand the hopes and dreams of our family members and students.

We live in a busy world, a place where it is all too easy to overlook the needs of others, but God's Word instructs us to do otherwise. In the Gospel of Matthew, Jesus declares, "In everything, therefore, treat people the same way you want them to treat you, for this is the Law and the Prophets" (Matthew 7:12 NASB).

Today, as you consider all the things that Christ has done in your life, honor Him by being a little kinder than necessary. Honor Christ by slowing down long enough to notice the trials and tribulations of your students. Honor Christ by giving the gift of understanding to friends and family. As a believer who has been eternally blessed by a loving Savior, you should do no less.

Whatever God does, the first outburst is
always compassion.

MEISTER ECKHART

Compassion will cure more sins than condemnation.

HENRY WARD BEECHER

Our actions are seen by people,
but our motives are monitored by God.

FRANKLIN GRAHAM

Let my heart be broken by the things
that break the heart of God.

BOB PIERCE

Before you can dry another's tears,
you too must weep.

BARBARA JOHNSON

MORE FROM GOD'S WORD

Create in me a pure heart, God,
and make my spirit right again.

PSALM 51:10 NCV

Every way of a man is right in his own eyes,
but the LORD weighs the hearts.

PROVERBS 21:2 NKJV

TODAY, I WILL THINK ABOUT . . .

The need to be an understanding mentor
to my students.

A PRAYER TO START MY DAY

Lord, make me a loving, encouraging,
compassionate Christian. And, let my love
for Christ be reflected through the kindness that
I show to my family, to my friends, to my students.
and to all who need the healing touch of
the Master's hand. ««Amen

THE WORDS YOU SPEAK TODAY

FROM A WISE MIND COMES WISE SPEECH;
THE WORDS OF THE WISE ARE PERSUASIVE.

PROVERBS 16:23 NLT

Think . . . pause . . . then speak: How wise is the teacher who can communicate in this way. But occasionally, amid the pressures of the school day, even the most considerate teacher may speak first and think next . . . with unfortunate results.

God's Word reminds us that "Reckless words pierce like a sword, but the tongue of the wise brings healing" (Proverbs 12:18 NIV) If we seek to be a source of encouragement to our students, to our peers, and to our families, then we must measure our words carefully. Words are important: they can hurt or heal. Words can uplift us or discourage us, and reckless words, spoken in haste, cannot be erased.

Today, seek to encourage all who cross your path. Measure your words carefully. Speak wisely, not impulsively. Use words of kindness and praise, not words of anger or derision. Remember that you have the power to heal others or to injure them, to lift others up or to hold them back. When you lift them up, your wisdom will bring healing and comfort to a classroom and a world that needs both.

Fill the heart with the love of Christ so that
only truth and purity can come out of the mouth.

WARREN WIERSBE

Perhaps we have been guilty of speaking against
someone and have not realized how it may have
hurt them. Then when someone speaks against us,
we suddenly realize how deeply such words hurt,
and we become sensitive to what we have done.

THEODORE EPP

In all your deeds and words, you should look on
Jesus as your model, whether you are keeping silence
or speaking, whether you are alone or with others.

ST. BONAVENTURE

Attitude and the spirit in which we communicate
are as important as the words we say.

CHARLES STANLEY

Happy the man whose words issue from
the Holy Spirit and not from himself.

ANTHONY OF PADUA

MORE FROM GOD'S WORD

Let your speech be alway with grace . . . .

COLOSSIANS 4:6 KJV

How forcible are right words!

JOB 6:25 KJV

TODAY, I WILL THINK ABOUT . . .

The importance of measuring my words carefully,
especially when I'm angry.

A PRAYER TO START MY DAY

Lord, You have commanded me to choose
my words carefully so that I might be a source of
encouragement and hope to all whom I meet.
Keep me mindful, Father, that I have influence
on many people, especially my students . . .
make me an influence for good. And may the words
that I speak today be worthy of the One
who has saved me forever. ««Amen

USING YOUR TALENTS TODAY

GOD HAS GIVEN EACH OF US THE ABILITY TO
DO CERTAIN THINGS WELL. SO IF GOD HAS
GIVEN YOU THE ABILITY TO PROPHESY,
SPEAK OUT WHEN YOU HAVE FAITH
THAT GOD IS SPEAKING THROUGH YOU.
IF YOUR GIFT IS THAT OF SERVING OTHERS,
SERVE THEM WELL. IF YOU ARE A TEACHER,
DO A GOOD JOB OF TEACHING. IF YOUR GIFT IS
TO ENCOURAGE OTHERS, DO IT! IF YOU HAVE
MONEY, SHARE IT GENEROUSLY. IF GOD HAS
GIVEN YOU LEADERSHIP ABILITY,
TAKE THE RESPONSIBILITY SERIOUSLY.
AND IF YOU HAVE A GIFT FOR SHOWING
KINDNESS TO OTHERS, DO IT GLADLY.

ROMANS 12:6-8 NLT

As a teacher, your profession places you in a position of profound responsibility: you help mold the minds and lives of your students. Daniel Webster wrote:

If we work in marble, it will perish; if we work upon brass, time will efface it; if we rear temples, they will crumble into dust; but if we work upon immortal minds and instill in them just principles, we are then engraving upon tablets which no time will efface, but which will brighten and brighten to all eternity.

These words point out the opportunities that are available to talented teachers like you. And make no mistake—God knew precisely what He was doing when He gave you a unique set of talents and opportunities. And now, God wants you to use those talents for the glory of His kingdom. So here's the big question: will you choose to use those talents, or not?

Being a godly teacher in today's difficult world requires insight, discipline, patience, and prayer. May you, with God's help, use your talents to touch the hearts and minds of your students and, in doing so, refashion this wonderful world . . . and the next.

Natural abilities are like natural plants;
they need pruning by study.

FRANCIS BACON

One thing taught large in the Holy Scriptures is
that while God gives His gifts freely, He will require
a strict accounting of them at the end of the road.
Each man is personally responsible for his store,
be it large or small, and will be required to explain
his use of it before the judgment seat of Christ.

A. W. TOZER

What greater work is there than training
the mind and forming the habits of the young?

ST. JOHN CHRYSOSTOM

Their little minds had a thousand hands reaching
and grabbing for everything they could see
(not unlike their physical hands). A parent-teacher's
job is to guide as much as possible what the hands of
their minds grab and store.

BETH MOORE

MORE FROM GOD'S WORD

The man who had received the five talents brought
the other five. "Master," he said, "you entrusted me
with five talents. See, I have gained five more."
His master replied, "Well done, good and faithful
servant! You have been faithful with a few things;
I will put you in charge of many things.
Come and share your master's happiness."

MATTHEW 25:20-21 NIV

TODAY, I WILL THINK ABOUT . . .

Ways that I can convert my talents into results.

A PRAYER TO START MY DAY

Heavenly Father, Your Word tells us that teachers
are judged strictly and that I have an awesome
responsibility to lead my students in the way of
truth. Lord, I ask for Your help today as I prepare
to teach. May I speak the truth, may I be a worthy
example to those who watch my behavior, and may
the glory be Yours. ««Amen

THE POWER OF A POSITIVE ATTITUDE

AND NOW, DEAR BROTHERS AND SISTERS,
LET ME SAY ONE MORE THING AS I CLOSE
THIS LETTER. FIX YOUR THOUGHTS ON
WHAT IS TRUE AND HONORABLE AND RIGHT.
THINK ABOUT THINGS THAT ARE PURE AND
LOVELY AND ADMIRABLE. THINK ABOUT THINGS
THAT ARE EXCELLENT AND WORTHY OF PRAISE.

PHILIPPIANS 4:8 NLT

A s the leader of your classroom, you must beware: your attitudes are contagious. If you're upbeat and optimistic, your students will tend to emulate you. But, if you fall prey to cynicism or pessimism, many of your students will, too.

How will you direct your thoughts today? Will you obey the words of Philippians 4:8 by dwelling upon those things that are true, honorable, and right? Or will you allow your thoughts to be hijacked by the negativity that seems to dominate our troubled world? Are you fearful, angry, bored, or worried? Are you so preoccupied with the concerns of this day that you fail to thank God for the promise of eternity? Are you confused, bitter, or pessimistic? If so, God wants to have a little talk with you.

God intends that you experience joy and abundance, but He will not force His joy upon you; you must claim it for yourself. So, today and every day hereafter, focus your thoughts and your energies upon "whatever is commendable."

Developing a positive attitude means working
continually to find what is uplifting and
encouraging.

BARBARA JOHNSON

If our hearts have been attuned to God through
an abiding faith in Christ, the result will be
joyous optimism and good cheer.

BILLY GRAHAM

The game was to just find something about
everything to be glad about—no matter what it was.
You see, when you're hunting for the glad things,
you sort of forget the other kind.

ELEANOR H. PORTER

Stop thinking wishfully and start living hopefully.

EMILIE BARNES

At least ten times every day, affirm this thought:
"I expect the best and, with God's help,
will attain the best."

NORMAN VINCENT PEALE

MORE FROM GOD'S WORD

*My cup runs over. Surely goodness and mercy
shall follow me all the days of my life;
and I will dwell in the house of the LORD Forever.*

PSALM 23:5-6 NKJV

*But if we look forward to something we don't have yet,
we must wait patiently and confidently.*

ROMANS 8:25 NLT

TODAY, I WILL THINK ABOUT . . .

The impact that my attitude has upon my students.

A PRAYER TO START MY DAY

Lord, give me faith, optimism, and hope.
Let me expect the best from You, and let me look for
the best in my students. Let me trust You, Lord,
to direct my life. And, let me be
Your faithful, hopeful, optimistic servant
every day that I live. ««Amen

BEING AN OBEDIENT SERVANT

JESUS ANSWERED, "IF PEOPLE LOVE ME,
THEY WILL OBEY MY TEACHING.
MY FATHER WILL LOVE THEM,
AND WE WILL COME TO THEM AND
MAKE OUR HOME WITH THEM."

JOHN 14:23 NCV

As concerned teachers, we must instruct our children to obey the rules of our classroom, the rules of society, and the laws of God. God's laws are contained in a guidebook for righteous living called the Holy Bible. It contains thorough instructions which, if followed, lead to fulfillment, peace, righteousness, and salvation. But, if we choose to ignore God's commandments, the results are as predictable as they are tragic.

Talking about obedience is easy; living obediently is considerably harder. But, if we are to be responsible role models for our families and students, we must study God's Word and obey it.

Talking about God is easy; living by His commandments is considerably harder. But, unless we are willing to abide by God's laws, all of our righteous proclamations ring hollow. So how can we best proclaim our love for the Lord? By obeying Him. And, for further instructions, read the manual.

God is God. Because He is God, He is worthy
of my trust and obedience. I will find rest nowhere
but in His holy will, a will that is unspeakably
beyond my largest notions of what He is up to.

ELISABETH ELLIOT

A life of obedience is not a life of following
a list of do's and don'ts, but it is allowing God
to be original in our lives.

VONETTE Z. BRIGHT

We offend God if we feel that he is cheating us out
of life, as if obeying him were a fast rather than
a feast. Obedience is a privilege not granted to
everyone. After all, God "comes to the help"
of obedient people.

RAYMOND ORTLUND

When we choose deliberately to obey Him,
then He will tax the remotest star and the last grain
of sand to assist us with all His almighty power.

OSWALD CHAMBERS

MORE FROM GOD'S WORD

*Anyone who listens to my teaching and obeys me is
wise, like a person who builds a house on solid rock.
Though the rain comes in torrents and the floodwaters
rise and the winds beat against that house,
it won't collapse, because it is built on rock.*

MATTHEW 7:24–25 NLT

TODAY, I WILL THINK ABOUT . . .

The blessings that I receive when I obey
God's commandments.

A PRAYER TO START MY DAY

Dear Lord, when I obey Your commandments, and
when I trust the promises of Your Son, I experience
love, peace, and abundance. Direct my path far from
the temptations and distractions of this world.
And, let me discover Your will and follow it,
dear Lord, this day and always. ««Amen

THE POWER OF PERSEVERANCE

LET US NOT BECOME WEARY IN DOING GOOD,
FOR AT THE PROPER TIME WE WILL
REAP A HARVEST IF WE DO NOT GIVE UP.

GALATIANS 6:9 NIV

The familiar saying is true: "Life is a marathon, not a sprint." And, the same can be said of the teaching profession. Teaching requires determination, especially on those difficult days when the students are in an uproar and the lesson plan is in disarray.

In a world filled with roadblocks and stumbling blocks, we need strength, courage, and perseverance. And, as an example of perfect perseverance, we need look no further than our Savior, Jesus Christ. Our Savior finished what He began, and so must we.

Perhaps you are in a hurry for God to reveal His unfolding plans for your life. If so, be forewarned: God operates on His own timetable, not yours. Sometimes, God may answer your prayers with silence, and when He does, you must patiently persevere. In times of trouble, you must remain steadfast and trust in the merciful goodness of your Heavenly Father. Whatever your challenge, God can handle it. Your job is to keep persevering until He does.

Failure is one of life's most powerful teachers.
How we handle our failures determines whether
we're going to simply "get by" in life or "press on."

BETH MOORE

Only the man who follows the command of
Jesus single-mindedly and unresistingly lets his yoke
rest upon him, finds his burden easy, and under
its gentle pressure receives the power to
persevere in the right way.

DIETRICH BONHOEFFER

That is the source of Jeremiah's living persistence,
his creative constancy. He was up before the sun,
listening to God's word. Rising early, he was quiet
and attentive before his Lord. Long before
the yelling started, the mocking, the complaining,
there was this centering, discovering,
exploring time with God.

EUGENE PETERSON

MORE FROM GOD'S WORD

*Thanks be to God! He gives us the victory through
our Lord Jesus Christ. Therefore, my dear brothers,
stand firm. Let nothing move you. Always give
yourselves fully to the work of the Lord, because
you know that your labor in the Lord is not in vain.*

1 CORINTHIANS 15:57-58 NIV

TODAY, I WILL THINK ABOUT . . .

The need for perseverance and courage.

A PRAYER TO START MY DAY

Heavenly Father, sometimes, this life is difficult
indeed. Sometimes, I am fearful. Sometimes,
I cry tears of bitterness and loss, but even then,
You never leave my side. Today, Lord, let me be
a finisher of my faith. Let me persevere—
even if the day is difficult—and let me follow
Your Son Jesus this day and forever. ««Amen

SHARING THE JOY

I WILL THANK THE LORD WITH ALL MY HEART;
I WILL DECLARE ALL YOUR WONDERFUL
WORKS. I WILL REJOICE AND BOAST
ABOUT YOU; I WILL SING ABOUT YOUR NAME,
MOST HIGH.

PSALM 9:1-2 HCSB

As you plan for the upcoming day, are you making plans to celebrate? Hopefully so. After all, teaching can and should be a joyful experience. But as every veteran teacher knows, some days are more challenging than others. Nevertheless, even on the most difficult days, we can find pockets of satisfaction, islands of peace, and moments of joy.

Oswald Chambers correctly observed, "Joy is the great note all throughout the Bible." C. S. Lewis echoed that thought when he wrote, "Joy is the serious business of heaven."

Today, resolve to be a joyful Christian with a smile on your face and a song in your heart. After all, this is God's day, and He has given us clear instructions for its use. We are commanded to rejoice and be glad. So, with no further ado, let the celebration begin . . . .

Better to instruct a child than to collect riches.

ST. HERVE OF BRITTANY

Teaching is a divine calling. Whether we teach
at home, at church, or in a school classroom,
transfer of knowledge is a significant undertaking.

SUZANNE DALE EZELL

The chief end of man is to glorify God and
enjoy him forever.

WESTMINSTER SHORTER CATECHISM

Christian joy is a gift from God flowing from
a good conscience.

ST. PHILIP NERI

The Christian should be an alleluia from
head to foot!

ST. AUGUSTINE

MORE FROM GOD'S WORD

Shout for joy to the LORD, all the earth.
Worship the LORD with gladness;
come before him with joyful songs.

PSALM 100:1-2 NIV

You will teach me how to live a holy life.
Being with you will fill me with joy; at your right hand
I will find pleasure forever.

PSALM 16:11 NCV

TODAY, I WILL THINK ABOUT . . .

All the blessings that God has given me.

A PRAYER TO START MY DAY

Lord, make me a joyous Christian. Because of
my salvation through Your Son, I have every reason
to celebrate—let my joy be evident in every aspect
of life, including my life inside the classroom.
Today, let my words and deeds be a testimony to
Christ's love and to His grace. ««Amen

WHAT KIND OF LEADER WILL YOU BE TODAY?

LOVE AND TRUTH FORM A GOOD LEADER;
SOUND LEADERSHIP IS FOUNDED
ON LOVING INTEGRITY.

PROVERBS 20:28 MSG

As a teacher, you are automatically placed in a position of leadership. Unless, you assume firm control over your students, effective learning will not take place in your classroom.

John Maxwell writes, "Great leaders understand that the right attitude will set the right atmosphere, which enables the right response from others." As the leader of your class, it's up to you to set the proper balance between discipline and amusement, between entertainment and scholarship.

Savvy teachers learn to strike an appropriate balance between discipline (which is necessary for maintaining order) and fun (which is necessary for maintaining interest). The rest, of course, is up to the students.

What kind of leader will you be today? Will you be the kind of teacher whose class you would want to attend if you were a student? Hopefully so, because our world always needs another competent, Christ-centered leader . . . and so, for that matter, do your students.

The goal of leadership is to empower
the whole people of God to discern and
to discharge the Lord's will.

STANLEY GRENZ

Leadership is found in becoming the servant of all.

RICHARD FOSTER

A Christian leader will succeed if she convinces
her followers that God—as well as she herself—
recognizes and honors the person's strengths
and abilities, and that each worker has
something of value to offer others.

LINDA MCGINN

You can never separate a leader's actions
from his character.

JOHN MAXWELL

A good leader is not the person who
does things right, but the one who finds
the right things to do.

ANTHONY T. PADOVANO

MORE FROM GOD'S WORD

*Those who are wise will shine like the brightness of
the heavens, and those who lead many to righteousness,
like the stars for ever and ever.*

DANIEL 12:3 NIV

*But a good leader plans to do good,
and those good things make him a good leader.*

ISAIAH 32:8 NCV

TODAY, I WILL THINK ABOUT . . .

The importance of being a Christ-centered leader.

A PRAYER TO START MY DAY

Dear Lord, let me be a leader in my classroom and
a worthy example to my students. Give me wisdom,
courage, compassion, and faith. Let me turn to You,
Father, for guidance and for strength
in all that I say and do. ««Amen

HAPPINESS NOW

BUT HAPPY ARE THOSE . . .
WHOSE HOPE IS IN THE LORD THEIR GOD.

PSALM 146:5 NLT

Do you seek happiness, abundance, and contentment? And do you seek these things now, not later? If so, here's what you should do: Love God and His Son; depend upon God for strength; try, to the best of your abilities, to follow God's will; and strive to obey His Holy Word. When you do these things, you'll discover that happiness goes hand-in-hand with righteousness.

Happiness depends less upon our circumstances than upon our thoughts. When we turn our thoughts to God, to His gifts, and to His glorious creation, we experience the joy that God intends for His children. But, when we focus on the negative aspects of life, we suffer needlessly.

Do you sincerely want to be a happy Christian? Then set your mind and your heart upon God's love and His grace. The fullness of life in Christ is available to all who seek it and claim it. Count yourself among that number. Seek first the salvation that is available through a personal relationship with Jesus Christ, and then claim the joy, the peace, and the spiritual abundance that the Shepherd offers His sheep.

If you want to be truly happy, you won't find it
on an endless quest for more stuff. You'll find it
in receiving God's generosity and then passing
that generosity along.

BILL HYBELS

Happiness is obedience, and obedience is happiness.

C. H. SPURGEON

Until your purpose lines up with God's purpose,
you will never be happy or fulfilled.

CHARLES STANLEY

If happiness is brought to others,
our own happiness is reflected.

FATHER FLANAGAN

There is no happiness in having, or in getting,
but only in giving.

HENRY DRUMMOND

MORE FROM GOD'S WORD

Obey God and be at peace with him;
this is the way to happiness.

JOB 22:21 NCV

For the happy heart, life is a continual feast.

PROVERBS 15:15 NLT

TODAY, I WILL THINK ABOUT . . .

The happiness and abundance that can be mine
when I obey God's commandments.

A PRAYER TO START MY DAY

Lord, let me be a teacher who celebrates life.
Let me rejoice in the gift of this day,
and let me praise You for the gift of Your Son.
Let me be a joyful Christian, Lord, as I share
Your Good News with friends, with family,
and with the world. ««Amen

MENTORING 101

FIX THESE WORDS OF MINE IN YOUR HEARTS
AND MINDS. TEACH THEM TO YOUR CHILDREN,
TALKING ABOUT THEM WHEN YOU SIT AT HOME
AND WHEN YOU WALK ALONG THE ROAD,
WHEN YOU LIE DOWN AND WHEN YOU GET UP.

DEUTERONOMY 11:18-19 NIV

Do you wish to become a better teacher and a wiser person? Then you must walk with people who, by their words and their presence, make you wiser. But that's not all; you must avoid those people who encourage you to think foolish thoughts or do foolish things.

Today, as a gift to yourself, select, from your friends and coworkers, a mentor whose judgement you trust. Then listen carefully to your mentor's advice and be willing to accept that advice, even if accepting it requires effort or pain, or both. Consider your mentor to be God's gift to you. Thank God for that gift, and treasure the wisdom that you gain.

And what should you do with all that hard-earned knowledge that you acquire from your mentor? Share it, of course, with the students and co-workers who are wise enough to learn from you.

Do not open your heart to every man,
but discuss your affairs with one who is
wise and who fears God.

THOMAS À KEMPIS

It takes a wise person to give good advice,
but an even wiser person to take it.

MARIE T. FREEMAN

Yes, the Spirit was sent to be our Counselor.
Yes, Jesus speaks to us personally.
But often he works through another human being.

JOHN ELDREDGE

The effective mentor strives to help a man or
woman discover what they can be in Christ and
then holds them accountable to
become that person.

HOWARD HENDRICKS

The man who never reads will never be read;
he who never quotes will never be quoted.
He who will not use the thoughts of other men's
brains proves that he has no brains of his own.

C. H. SPURGEON

MORE FROM GOD'S WORD

A wise man will hear and increase in learning,
and a man of understanding will acquire wise counsel.

PROVERBS 1:5 NASB

Get all the advice and instruction you can,
and be wise the rest of your life.

PROVERBS 19:20 NLT

TODAY, I WILL THINK ABOUT . . .

Ways that I can share my wisdom with my students,
my friends, and my family.

A PRAYER TO START MY DAY

Lord, make me a wise counselor to those whom
I teach. Make me a worthy mentor and a godly
example to my students. Let me lead them in the
ways of wisdom, discipline, and righteousness by
the words that I speak and the way that
I live my life. ««Amen

TEACHING INTEGRITY

GOOD LEADERS CULTIVATE HONEST SPEECH.

PROVERBS 16:13 MSG

From the time we are children, we are taught that honesty is the best policy. And, in the classroom, we instruct our students that honesty is also the school's policy. But, honesty is not just the best policy or the school's policy, it is also God's policy. If we are to be servants worthy of His blessings, we must remember that truth is not just the best way; it is God's way.

Wise teachers understand the importance of character . . . and teach it. Character is built slowly over a lifetime. It is the sum of every right decision, every honest word, every noble thought, and every heartfelt prayer. It is forged on the anvil of honorable work and polished by the twin virtues of generosity and humility. Character is a precious thing—difficult to build, but easy to tear down; godly teachers value it and protect it at all costs . . . and they encourage their students to do the same.

Maintaining your integrity in a world of sham
is no small accomplishment.

WAYNE OATES

Persons of true character are neither
optimists nor pessimists,
but realists who have confidence in God.

WARREN WIERSBE

Character is both developed and revealed by tests,
and all of life is a test.

RICK WARREN

Jesus—the standard of measurement,
the scale of weights, the test of character
for the whole moral universe.

R. G. LEE

Character is made in the small moments of our lives.

PHILLIPS BROOKS

MORE FROM GOD'S WORD

*In all things showing yourself to be a pattern
of good works; in doctrine showing integrity,
reverence, incorruptibility . . . .*

TITUS 2:7 NKJV

*We also rejoice in our sufferings, because we know
that suffering produces perseverance; perseverance,
character; and character, hope.*

ROMANS 5:3-4 NIV

TODAY, I WILL THINK ABOUT . . .

Ways that I can remove myself from situations
that might compromise my integrity.

A PRAYER TO START MY DAY

Heavenly Father, Your Word instructs me to walk
in integrity and in truth. Make me a worthy teacher,
Lord. Let my words be true, and let my actions
lead my students to You. ««Amen

THE WISDOM TO FORGIVE

BE KIND AND LOVING TO EACH OTHER,

AND FORGIVE EACH OTHER

JUST AS GOD FORGAVE YOU IN CHRIST.

EPHESIANS 4:32 NCV

E ven the most mild-mannered teachers will, on occasion, have reason to become angry with the inevitable shortcomings of students. But wise teachers are quick to forgive others, just as God has forgiven them.

Teachers, having been placed in positions of leadership, serve as important role models to their students. As such, teachers must be models of forgiveness, both inside the classroom and out.

Are you easily frustrated by the inevitable shortcomings of others? Are you a prisoner of bitterness or regret? If so, perhaps you need a refresher course in the art of forgiveness.

So, if there exists even one person, alive or dead, whom you have not forgiven (and that includes yourself), follow God's commandment and His will for your life: forgive. Hatred and bitterness and regret are not part of God's plan for your life. Forgiveness is.

Jesus is the only One who makes not only our sins
but also the sins of others against us forgivable.

ANNE GRAHAM LOTZ

Doing an injury puts you below your enemy;
revenging an injury makes you even with him;
forgiving an injury sets you above him!

ANONYMOUS

Forgiveness enables you to bury your grudge in
icy earth. To put the past behind you.
To flush resentment away by being the first to
forgive. Forgiveness fashions your future.
It is a brave and brash thing to do.

BARBARA JOHNSON

In praying for people one dislikes I find it helpful to
remember that one is joining in His prayer for them.

C. S. LEWIS

Every time we forgive others, deserving it or not,
we have a reminder of God's forgiveness.

FRANKLIN GRAHAM

MORE FROM GOD'S WORD

*Be even-tempered, content with second place,
quick to forgive an offense. Forgive as quickly and
completely as the Master forgave you.
And regardless of what else you put on, wear love.
It's your basic, all-purpose garment.
Never be without it.*

COLOSSIANS 3:13-14 MSG

TODAY, I WILL THINK ABOUT . . .

The people whom I still need to forgive.

A PRAYER TO START MY DAY

Heavenly Father, sometimes I am tempted to
strike out at those who have hurt me. Keep me
mindful that forgiveness is Your commandment.
You have forgiven me, Lord; let me show
my thankfulness to You by offering forgiveness to
others. And, when I do, may others see Your love
reflected through my words and deeds. ««Amen

BELIEVING IN YOUR STUDENTS

LET'S SEE HOW INVENTIVE WE CAN BE
IN ENCOURAGING LOVE AND HELPING OUT,
NOT AVOIDING WORSHIPPING TOGETHER AS
SOME DO BUT SPURRING EACH OTHER ON.

HEBREWS 10:24-25 MSG

For young people experiencing life here in the new Millennium, the world can be a difficult and uncertain place. Many of our students are in desperate need of a smile or an encouraging word, and since we don't always know who needs our help, the best strategy is to encourage all those who cross our paths.

Great teachers encourage impressionable students to believe in themselves. Great teachers inspire confidence. Great teachers encourage their students to learn, to work, to grow, and to persevere.

So, as you make plans for the upcoming day, promise yourself that you'll be the kind of teacher who encourages students to believe in themselves. Never has the need been greater.

If someone listens or stretches out a hand or
whispers a word of encouragement or
attempts to understand a lonely person,
extraordinary things begin to happen.

LORETTA GIRZARTIS

What sunshine is to flowers, smiles are to humanity.
They are but trifles scattered to humanity.
They are but trifles scattered along life's pathway,
but the good they do is inconceivable.

JOSEPH ADDISON

Good, the more communicated,
more abundant grows.

JOHN MILTON

One of the sanest, surest, and most generous joys of
life comes from being happy over
the good fortune of others.

ARCHIBALD RUTLEDGE

How many people stop because so few say, "Go!"

CHARLES SWINDOLL

MORE FROM GOD'S WORD

Good people's words will help many others.

PROVERBS 10:21 NCV

TODAY, I WILL THINK ABOUT . . .

Ways that I can be a positive influence
on my students.

A PRAYER TO START MY DAY

Dear Lord, You have loved me eternally, and
cared for me faithfully. Just as You have lifted me
up, Lord, let me also lift up others in a spirit of
encouragement, optimism, and hope.
Today and every day, let me share Your healing
message so that I might encourage others.
And, Lord, may the glory be Yours. ««Amen

WHEN THE DAY IS DIFFICULT

GOD BLESSES THE PEOPLE WHO
PATIENTLY ENDURE TESTING.
AFTERWARD THEY WILL RECEIVE
THE CROWN OF LIFE THAT GOD
HAS PROMISED TO THOSE WHO LOVE HIM.

JAMES 1:12 NLT

Teachers of every generation have experienced challenges, and this generation is no different. But, today's teachers face difficulties that previous generations could have scarcely imagined. Thankfully, although the world continues to change, God's love remains constant. And, He remains ready to comfort us and strengthen us whenever we turn to Him.

Because we human beings have the ability to think, we also have the ability to worry. All of us, even the most faithful believers, are plagued by occasional periods of discouragement and doubt. Even though we hold tightly to God's promise of salvation—even though we believe sincerely in God's love and protection—we may find ourselves fretting over the countless details of everyday life. We worry about health, about finances, about safety, about relationships, about family, and about countless other challenges, some great and some small.

Where is the best place to take our worries? We should take them to God. We should take our troubles to Him, and our fears, our dilemmas and our sorrows. We should seek protection from the One who cannot be moved. Then, when we have genuinely turned our concerns over to God, we should worry less and trust Him more, because God is trustworthy . . . and we are protected.

Love accepts the trying things of life without
asking for explanations. It trusts and is at rest.

AMY CARMICHAEL

If we had no winter, the spring would not be
so pleasant; if we did not sometimes taste of
adversity, prosperity would not be so welcome.

ANNE BRADSTREET

Growth in depth and strength and consistency and
fruitfulness and ultimately in Christlikeness is
only possible when the winds of life are
contrary to personal comfort.

ANNE GRAHAM LOTZ

Life is simply hard. That's all there is to it.
Thank goodness, the intensity of difficulty rises
and falls. Some seasons are far more bearable than
others but none is without challenge.

BETH MOORE

Whatever hallway you're in—
no matter how long, how dark, or how scary—
God is right there with you.

BILL HYBELS

MORE FROM GOD'S WORD

When you go through deep waters and great trouble,
I will be with you. When you go through the rivers of
difficulty, you will not drown! When you walk through
the fire of oppression, you will not be burned up;
the flames will not consume you.
For I am the LORD, your God . . . .

ISAIAH 43:2-3 NLT

TODAY, I WILL THINK ABOUT . . .

The comfort and strength that can be mine
when I open my heart to God.

A PRAYER TO START MY DAY

Heavenly Father, You are my strength and refuge.
I can face the difficulties of this day because
You are with me. You are my light and pathway.
As I follow You, Father, I can overcome adversity
just as Jesus overcame this world. ««Amen

WHOM WILL YOU SERVE TODAY?

WHOEVER WANTS TO BECOME GREAT
AMONG YOU MUST SERVE
THE REST OF YOU LIKE A SERVANT.

MATTHEW 20:26 NCV

Jesus teaches that the most esteemed men and women are not the leaders of society or the captains of industry. To the contrary, Jesus teaches that the greatest among us are those who choose to minister and to serve.

When you decided to become a teacher, you chose a life of service. Congratulations! Your kindness and generosity will touch the lives of students in ways that you will never fully comprehend. But God knows the impact of your good works, and He will bless you because of them.

The words of Galatians 6:9 are clear: "Let us not become weary in doing good, for at the proper time we will reap a harvest if we do not give up" (NIV). May you never grow weary of your role as a teacher, and may your good works continue to bless your students long after the final school bell has rung.

The man who walks with God always gets
to his destination.

HENRIETTA MEARS

Through our service to others,
God wants to influence our world for Him.

VONETTE BRIGHT

We have to serve God in His way, not in ours.

ST. TERESA OF AVILA

Service is the pathway to real significance.

RICK WARREN

Come work for the Lord. The work is hard,
the hours are long, and the pay is low,
but the retirement benefits are out of this world.

ANONYMOUS

MORE FROM GOD'S WORD

You address me as "Teacher" and "Master,"
and rightly so. That is what I am. So if I, the Master
and Teacher, washed your feet, you must now wash
each other's feet. I've laid down a pattern for you.
What I've done, you do.

JOHN 13:15 MSG

TODAY, I WILL THINK ABOUT . . .

Creative ways that I can serve my students.

A PRAYER TO START MY DAY

Lord, I can serve only one master; let me serve You.
Let my actions be pleasing to You; let my words
reflect Your infinite love; let my prayers be sincere
and my thoughts be pure. In everything that I do,
Father, let me praise You and serve You
today and for eternity. ««Amen

TRUSTING HIM TODAY

AS FOR GOD, HIS WAY IS PERFECT;

THE WORD OF THE LORD IS PROVEN;

HE IS A SHIELD TO ALL WHO TRUST IN HIM.

PSALM 18:30 NKJV

Sometimes your future seems bright, and sometimes it does not. Yet even when you cannot see the possibilities of tomorrow, God can. Your challenge is to trust an uncertain future to an all-powerful God.

When you trust God, you should trust Him without reservation. You should steel yourself against the inevitable disappointments of today, secure in the knowledge that your Heavenly Father has a plan for the future that only He can see. But sometimes trusting God is hard, especially when you face the inevitable disappointments and hardships of life here on earth.

Are you willing to place extreme trust in God? Hopefully so, because sooner or later, you'll need it. On occasion, you will confront circumstances that trouble you to the very core of your soul. When you are afraid, trust in God. When you are worried, turn your concerns over to Him. When you are anxious, be still and listen for the quiet assurance of God's promises. And then, place your life in His hands. He is your shepherd today and throughout eternity. Trust the Shepherd.

Ten thousand enemies cannot stop a Christian,
cannot even slow him down, if he meets them
in an attitude of complete trust in God.

A. W. TOZER

If God has called you to run through a wall,
your job is to take off running and trust
that a hole will be there just as you get there.

ANDY STANLEY

Only love empowers the leap in trust,
the courage to risk everything on Jesus,
the readiness to move into the darkness guided
only by a pillar of fire.

BRENNAN MANNING

Trust in yourself and you are doomed
to disappointment; trust in money and you may
have it taken from you, but trust in God,
and you are never to be confounded
in time or eternity.

D. L. MOODY

MORE FROM GOD'S WORD

Blessed is he that trusts in the LORD.

PROVERBS 16:20 NIV

Jesus overheard and said, "Don't be upset.
Just trust me and everything will be all right."

LUKE 8:50 MSG

TODAY, I WILL THINK ABOUT . . .

The importance of continuing to grow
in the knowledge and love of the Lord.

A PRAYER TO START MY DAY

Dear Lord, I come to You today with hope in my
heart and praise on my lips. I place my trust in You,
dear God, knowing that with You as my Protector,
I have nothing to fear. I thank You, Father,
for Your grace, for Your Love, and for Your Son.
Let me follow in Christ's footsteps today and
every day that I live. And then, when my work here
is done, let me live with You forever. ««Amen

LOVE ONE ANOTHER

I GIVE YOU A NEW COMMANDMENT:
THAT YOU LOVE ONE ANOTHER.
JUST AS I HAVE LOVED YOU, YOU SHOULD ALSO
LOVE ONE ANOTHER. BY THIS ALL PEOPLE
WILL KNOW THAT YOU ARE MY DISCIPLES,
IF YOU HAVE LOVE FOR ONE ANOTHER.

JOHN 13:34-35 HCSB

God loves you. How will you respond to His love? The Bible clearly defines what your response should be: "You shall love the Lord your God with all your heart, with all your soul, and with all your strength" (Deuteronomy 6:5 NKJV). But you must not stop there. You must also love your neighbor as yourself. Jesus teaches that "On these two commandments hang all the Law and the Prophets" (Matthew 22: 40).

Today, as you meet the demands of everyday living, will you pause long enough to return God's love? And then will you share it? Prayerfully, you will. When you embrace God's love, you are forever changed. When you embrace God's love, you feel differently about yourself, your family, your students, your friends, and your world. When you embrace God's love, you have enough love to keep and enough love to share: enough love for a day, enough love for a lifetime, enough love for all eternity.

God loves these people too; just because
they're unattractive or warped in their thinking
doesn't mean the Lord doesn't love them.
And if we don't take them,
who is going to take them?

RUTH BELL GRAHAM

You can be sure you are abiding in Christ
if you are able to have a Christlike love toward
the people that irritate you the most.

VONETTE BRIGHT

Love alone makes heavy burdens light and bears in
equal balance things pleasing and displeasing.
Love bears a heavy burden and does not feel it,
and love makes bitter things tasteful and sweet.

THOMAS À KEMPIS

To love another person is to help them love God.

SØREN KIERKEGAARD

There is no love which does not become help.

PAUL TILLICH

MORE FROM GOD'S WORD

Pay all your debts, except the debt of love for others.
You can never finish paying that! If you love your
neighbor, you will fulfill all the requirements
of God's law.

ROMANS 13:8 NLT

TODAY, I WILL THINK ABOUT . . .

Ways that I can use both words and deeds
to demonstrate the love that I feel
in my heart for others.

A PRAYER TO START MY DAY

Lord, You have given me love that is beyond human
understanding, and I am Your loving servant.
May the love that I feel for You be reflected in the
compassion that I show toward others. Give me
Your eyes to see others as You see them, Lord, and
let me be generous and kind to those who cross my
path this day and every day. ««Amen

THE POWER OF PRAYER

THE EARNEST PRAYER OF
A RIGHTEOUS PERSON HAS GREAT POWER
AND WONDERFUL RESULTS.

JAMES 5:16 NLT

"The power of prayer": these words are so familiar, yet sometimes we forget what they mean. Prayer is a powerful tool for communicating with our Creator; it is an opportunity to commune with the Giver of all things good. Prayer helps us find strength for today and hope for the future. Prayer is a tool we can use to help others. Prayer is not a thing to be taken lightly or to be used infrequently.

Is prayer an integral part of your life, or is it a hit-or-miss habit? Do you "pray without ceasing," or is your prayer life an afterthought? Do you regularly pray for your family, your friends, and your students . . . or do you bow your head only when others are watching?

The quality of your spiritual life will be in direct proportion to the quality of your prayer life. Prayer changes things, and it changes you. Today, instead of turning things over in your mind, turn them over to God in prayer. Instead of worrying about your next decision, ask God to lead the way. Don't limit your prayers to meals or to bedtime. Pray constantly about things great and small. God is listening, and He wants to hear from you now.

Prayer accomplishes more than anything else.

BILL BRIGHT

A little child cannot do a bad coloring;
nor can a child of God do a bad prayer.

BRENNAN MANNING

The Christian prays in every situation,
in his walks for recreation, in his dealing with
others, in silence, in reading, in all rational pursuits.

CLEMENT OF ALEXANDRIA

Nothing is clearer than that prayer has its
only worth and significance in the great fact
that God hears and answers prayer.

E. M. BOUNDS

The best reason to pray is that God is really there.
In praying, our unbelief gradually starts to melt
as God moves smack into the middle
of even an ordinary day.

EMILIE GRIFFIN

MORE FROM GOD'S WORD

Listen, listen to me, and eat what is good,
and your soul will delight in the richest of fare.
Give ear and come to me;
hear me, that your soul may live.

ISAIAH 55:2-3 NIV

TODAY, I WILL THINK ABOUT . . .

The role that prayer plays in my life.

A PRAYER TO START MY DAY

Lord, I pray to You because You desire it and
because I need it. Prayer not only changes things,
it also changes me. Help me, Lord, never to face
the demands of the day without first spending time
with You, and help me to make prayer
a part of everything that I do and
everything that I am. ««Amen

THE POWER OF POSITIVE TEACHING

GIVE YOUR WORRIES TO THE LORD,
AND HE WILL TAKE CARE OF YOU.
HE WILL NEVER LET GOOD PEOPLE DOWN.

PSALM 55:22 NCV

Christians have every reason to be optimistic about life. As Billy Graham observed, "Christ can put a spring in your step and a thrill in your heart. Optimism and cheerfulness are products of knowing Christ." But sometimes, when we are tired or frustrated, optimism and cheerfulness seem like distant promises. They are not. Thankfully, our God stands ready to restore us: "I will give you a new heart and put a new spirit in you . . ." (Ezekiel 36:26 NIV). Our task, of course, is to let Him.

Today, accept the new spirit that God seeks to infuse into your heart. Think optimistically about yourself, your students, your school, and your world. Rejoice in this glorious day that the Lord has given you, and share your optimism with your friends, with your co-workers, and with your students. Your enthusiasm will be contagious. And your words will bring healing and comfort to a world that needs both.

With the peace of God to guard us and
the God of peace to guide us—why worry?

WARREN WIERSBE

The closer you live to God,
the smaller everything else appears.

RICK WARREN

Refuse to be swamped by the cares of the world.

OSWALD CHAMBERS

Don't take tomorrow to bed with you.

NORMAN VINCENT PEALE

Never yield to gloomy anticipation.
Place your hope and confidence in God.
He has no record of failure.

MRS. CHARLES E. COWMAN

MORE FROM GOD'S WORD

Don't worry about anything, but in everything,
through prayer and petition with thanksgiving,
let your requests be made known to God.

PHILIPPIANS 4:6 HCSB

TODAY, I WILL THINK ABOUT . . .

The impact of my optimism on others.

A PRAYER TO START MY DAY

Lord, You sent Your Son to live as a man on this
earth, and You know what it means to be completely
human. You understand my worries and my fears,
Lord, and You forgive me when I am weak.
When my faith begins to wane, help me, Lord,
to trust You more. Then, with Your Holy Word on
my lips and with the love of Your Son in my heart,
let me live courageously, faithfully, prayerfully,
and thankfully today and every day. ««Amen

IN HIS FOOTSTEPS

WHOEVER SERVES ME MUST FOLLOW ME.
THEN MY SERVANT WILL BE WITH ME
EVERYWHERE I AM. MY FATHER WILL HONOR
ANYONE WHO SERVES ME.

JOHN 12:26 NCV

J esus walks with you. Are you walking with Him? Hopefully, you will choose to walk with Him today and every day of your life.

Jesus loved you so much that He endured unspeakable humiliation and suffering for you. How will you respond to Christ's sacrifice? Will you take up His cross and follow Him (Luke 9:23), or will you choose another path? When you place your hopes squarely at the foot of the cross, when you place Jesus squarely at the center of your life, you will be blessed.

The old familiar hymn begins, "What a friend we have in Jesus . . . ." No truer words were ever penned. Jesus is the sovereign Friend and ultimate Savior of mankind. Christ showed enduring love for His believers by willingly sacrificing His own life so that we might have eternal life. Now, it is our turn to become His friend.

Let us love our Savior, let us praise Him, and let us share His message of salvation with the world. When we do, we demonstrate that our acquaintance with the Master is not a passing fancy, but is, instead, the cornerstone and the touchstone of our lives.

You cannot cooperate with Jesus in becoming what
He wants you to become and simultaneously be
what the world desires to make you. If you would
say, "Take the world but give me Jesus," then
you must deny yourself and take up your cross.
The simple truth is that your "self" must be put to
death in order for you to get to the point where
for you to live is Christ. What will it be?
The world and you, or Jesus and you?
You do have a choice to make.

KAY ARTHUR

Christ tells us that if we want to join Him,
we will travel the way He took. Surely it is not right
that the Son of God should go His way on
the path of shame while the sons of men walk
the way of worldly honor.

JOHN OF AVILA

When we truly walk with God throughout our day,
life slowly starts to fall into place.

BILL HYBELS

MORE FROM GOD'S WORD

Then He said to them all,
"If anyone desires to come after Me, let him deny
himself, and take up his cross daily, and follow Me.
For whoever desires to save his life will lose it,
but whoever loses his life for My sake will save it."

LUKE 9:23-24 NKJV

TODAY, I WILL THINK ABOUT . . .

The joyful abundance that is mine
when I follow Christ..

A PRAYER TO START MY DAY

Dear Lord, You are my Teacher—I will study
Your Word, and I will seek Your will. Today, I will
stand upon the truth that You reveal, and I will
share Your wisdom with my family, with my friends,
with my students, and with the world. ««Amen

BIBLE VERSES
TO
CONSIDER

FEAR

For God has not given us a spirit of fear,
but of power and of love and of a sound mind.

2 TIMOTHY 1:7 NLT

Don't be afraid, because I am your God.
I will make you strong and will help you;
I will support you with my right hand that saves you.

ISAIAH 41:10 NCV

I leave you peace; my peace I give you.
I do not give it to you as the world does.
So don't let your hearts be troubled or afraid.

JOHN 14:27 NCV

So He said, "Come." And when Peter had come down
out of the boat, he walked on the water to go to Jesus.
But when he saw that the wind was boisterous,
he was afraid; and beginning to sink he cried out,
saying, "Lord, save me!" And immediately Jesus
stretched out His hand and caught him, and said to him,
"O you of little faith, why did you doubt?"
And when they got into the boat, the wind ceased.

MATTHEW 14:29-32 NKJV

DON'T BE AFRAID,
BECAUSE THE LORD YOUR GOD
WILL BE WITH YOU
EVERYWHERE YOU GO.

JOSHUA 1:9 NCV

FAMILY

*A kingdom that is divided cannot continue,
and a family that is divided cannot continue.*

MARK 3:24-25 NCV

*. . . these should learn first of all to put their religion
into practice by caring for their own family . . . .*

1 TIMOTHY 5:4 NIV

*Choose for yourselves today the one
you will worship . . . . As for me and my family,
we will worship the LORD.*

JOSHUA 24:15 HCSB

*Unless the LORD builds a house, its builders labor
over it in vain; unless the LORD watches over a city,
the watchman stays alert in vain.*

PSALM 127:1 HCSB

HE WHO BRINGS TROUBLE
ON HIS FAMILY WILL INHERIT
ONLY WIND . . . .

PROVERBS 11:29 NIV

ETERNAL LIFE

I assure you, anyone who believes in me
already has eternal life.

JOHN 6:47 NLT

Truly, truly, I say to you, he who hears My word,
and believes Him who sent Me, has eternal life,
and does not come into judgment, but has passed out
of death into life. Truly, truly, I say to you, an hour is
coming and now is, when the dead will hear the voice of
the Son of God, and those who hear will live.

JOHN 5:24-25 NASB

Jesus told this simple story, but they had no idea
what he was talking about. So he tried again.
"I'll be explicit, then. I am the Gate for the sheep.
All those others are up to no good—sheep stealers,
every one of them. But the sheep didn't listen to them.
I am the Gate. Anyone who goes through me will be
cared for—will freely go in and out, and find pasture.
A thief is only there to steal and kill and destroy.
I came so they can have real and eternal life,
more and better life than they ever dreamed of."

JOHN 10:6-10 MSG

For God so loved the world
that he gave his only Son,
so that everyone who believes
in him will not perish
but have eternal life.

John 3:16 NLT

DOUBT

*If you don't know what you're doing, pray to
the Father. He loves to help. You'll get his help,
and won't be condescended to when you ask for it.
Ask boldly, believingly, without a second thought. People
who "worry their prayers" are like wind-whipped waves.
Don't think you're going to get anything from the Master
that way, adrift at sea, keeping all your options open.*

JAMES 1:5-8 MSG

Purify your hearts, ye double-minded.

JAMES 4:8 KJV

*Immediately the father of the child cried out and
said with tears, "Lord, I believe; help my unbelief!"*

MARK 9:24 NKJV

*When doubts filled my mind,
your comfort gave me renewed hope and cheer.*

PSALM 94:19 NLT

AND IMMEDIATELY JESUS
STRETCHED FORTH HIS HAND,
AND CAUGHT HIM, AND SAID
UNTO HIM, O THOU OF LITTLE FAITH,
WHEREFORE DIDST THOU DOUBT?

MATTHEW 14:31 KJV

COURTESY

Out of respect for Christ,
be courteously reverent to one another.

EPHESIANS 5:21 MSG

Be hospitable to one another without grumbling.

1 PETER 4:9 NKJV

Are there those among you who are truly wise and
understanding? Then they should show it by
living right and doing good things with a gentleness
that comes from wisdom.

JAMES 3:13 NCV

A good person produces good deeds from a good heart,
and an evil person produces evil deeds from
an evil heart. Whatever is in your heart
determines what you say.

LUKE 6:45 NLT

DEAR FRIEND, WHEN YOU EXTEND
HOSPITALITY TO CHRISTIAN
BROTHERS AND SISTERS,
EVEN WHEN THEY ARE STRANGERS,
YOU MAKE THE FAITH VISIBLE.

3 JOHN 1:5 MSG

CONTENTMENT

Satisfy us in the morning with your unfailing love,
that we may sing for joy and be glad all our days.

PSALM 90:14 NIV

I am not saying this because I am in need,
for I have learned to be content whatever
the circumstances.

PHILIPPIANS 4:11 NIV

Keep your lives free from the love of money and
be content with what you have, because God has said,
"Never will I leave you; never will I forsake you."

HEBREWS 13:5 NIV

But godliness with contentment is great gain.
For we brought nothing into the world, and we can take
nothing out of it. But if we have food and clothing,
we will be content with that.

1 TIMOTHY 6:6-8 NIV

A HEART AT PEACE GIVES
LIFE TO THE BODY,
BUT ENVY ROTS THE BONES.

PROVERBS 14:30 NIV

CONSCIENCE

*So I strive always to keep my conscience clear
before God and man.*

ACTS 24:16 NIV

*Since, then, you have been raised with Christ,
set your hearts on things above, where Christ is seated at
the right hand of God. Set your minds on things above,
not on earthly things.*

COLOSSIANS 3:1-2 NIV

*Let us draw near to God with a sincere heart in
full assurance of faith, having our hearts sprinkled to
cleanse us from a guilty conscience and having
our bodies washed with pure water.*

HEBREWS 10:22 NIV

*Do not conform any longer to the pattern of this world,
but be transformed by the renewing of your mind.
Then you will be able to test and approve what
God's will is—his good, pleasing and perfect will.*

ROMANS 12:2 NIV

I WILL MAINTAIN
MY RIGHTEOUSNESS AND
NEVER LET GO OF IT;
MY CONSCIENCE WILL NOT
REPROACH ME AS LONG AS I LIVE.

JOB 27:6 NIV

BLESSINGS

So think clearly and exercise self-control.
Look forward to the special blessings that will
come to you at the return of Jesus Christ.

1 PETER 1:13 NLT

I pray also that you will have greater understanding in
your heart so you will know the hope to which he has
called us and that you will know how rich and glorious
are the blessings God has promised his holy people.
And you will know that God's power is
very great for us who believe.

EPHESIANS 1:18-19 NCV

I will make you into a great nation and I will bless you;
I will make your name great, and you will be a blessing.
I will bless those who bless you, and whoever curses you
I will curse; and all peoples on earth
will be blessed through you.

GENESIS 12:2-3 NIV

The LORD bless thee, and keep thee: The LORD make his
face shine upon thee, and be gracious unto thee.

NUMBERS 6:24-25 KJV

I WILL BLESS THEM AND
THE PLACES SURROUNDING
MY HILL. I WILL SEND DOWN
SHOWERS IN SEASON;
THERE WILL BE SHOWERS
OF BLESSINGS.

EZEKIEL 34:26 NIV

BEHAVIOR

*Yes, each of us will have to give
a personal account to God.*

ROMANS 14:12 NLT

*Let us walk properly, as in the day,
not in revelry and drunkenness, not in lewdness and
lust, not in strife and envy.*

ROMANS 13:13 NKJV

*Light shines on the godly, and joy on those who do right.
May all who are godly be happy in the LORD
and praise his holy name.*

PSALM 97:11-12 NLT

*Blessed is the man that walketh not in the counsel of
the ungodly, nor standeth in the way of sinners,
nor sitteth in the seat of the scornful.*

PSALM 1:1 KJV

A FOOL FINDS PLEASURE
IN EVIL CONDUCT,
BUT A MAN OF UNDERSTANDING
DELIGHTS IN WISDOM.

PROVERBS 10:23 NIV

ASKING GOD

Ask, and God will give to you. Search, and you will find. Knock, and the door will open for you. Yes, everyone who asks will receive. Everyone who searches will find. And everyone who knocks will have the door opened.

MATTHEW 7:7-8 NCV

Ask in my name, according to my will, and he'll most certainly give it to you. Your joy will be a river overflowing its banks!

JOHN 16:24 MSG

You did not choose me, but I chose you and appointed you to go and bear fruit—fruit that will last. Then the Father will give you whatever you ask in my name.

JOHN 15:16 NIV

You do not have, because you do not ask God.

JAMES 4:2 NIV

DO NOT WORRY ABOUT ANYTHING,
BUT PRAY AND ASK GOD FOR
EVERYTHING YOU NEED,
ALWAYS GIVING THANKS.

PHILIPPIANS 4:6 NCV

ARGUMENTS

*But stay away from those who have foolish arguments
and talk about useless family histories and argue and
quarrel about the law. Those things are worth
nothing and will not help anyone.*

TITUS 3:9 NCV

*Foolish people are always fighting,
but avoiding quarrels will bring you honor.*

PROVERBS 20:3 NCV

*Where do you think all these appalling wars and
quarrels come from? Do you think they just happen?
Think again. They come about because you want
your own way, and fight for it deep inside yourselves.*

JAMES 4:1 MSG

*God's servant must not be argumentative, but
a gentle listener and a teacher who keeps cool, working
firmly but patiently with those who refuse to obey.
You never know how or when God might sober them up
with a change of heart and a turning to the truth.*

2 TIMOTHY 2:24-25 MSG

DO EVERYTHING WITHOUT
GRUMBLING AND ARGUING,
SO THAT YOU MAY BE
BLAMELESS AND PURE.

PHILIPPIANS 2:14-15 HCSB

ANGER

Wise men turn away anger.

PROVERBS 29:8 NASB

Don't sin by letting anger gain control over you.
Think about it overnight and remain silent.

PSALM 4:4 NLT

Bad temper is contagious—don't get infected.

PROVERBS 22:25 MSG

But I tell you that anyone who is angry
with his brother is subject to judgment.

MATTHEW 5:22 NIV

My dearly loved brothers, understand this:
everyone must be quick to hear, slow to speak,
and slow to anger, for man's anger does not
accomplish God's righteousness.

JAMES 1:19-20 HCSB

TRUTH

Then you will know the truth,
and the truth will set you free.

JOHN 8:32 NIV

Teach me Your way, O LORD;
I will walk in Your truth.

PSALM 86:11 NASB

These are the things you are to do:
Speak the truth to each other, and render true and
sound judgment in your courts . . . .

ZECHARIAH 8:16 NIV

But when he, the Spirit of truth, comes,
he will guide you into all truth . . . .

JOHN 16:13 NIV

Jesus answered,
"I am the way and the truth and the life.
No one comes to the Father except through me."

JOHN 14:6 NIV

THANKSGIVING

If I eat what is served to me, grateful to God for what is on the table, how can I worry about what someone will say? I thanked God for it and he blessed it!

1 CORINTHIANS 10:30 MSG

Our prayers for you are always spilling over into thanksgivings. We can't quit thanking God our Father and Jesus our Messiah for you!

COLOSSIANS 1:3 MSG

Enter his gates with thanksgiving, go into his courts with praise. Give thanks to him and bless his name.

PSALM 100:4 NLT

I will give thanks to the LORD with all my heart; I will tell of all Your wonders. I will be glad and exult in You; I will sing praise to Your name, O Most High.

PSALM 9:1-2 NASB

THANKS BE TO GOD FOR
HIS INDESCRIBABLE GIFT!

2 CORINTHIANS 9:15 NIV

SIMPLICITY

*You've gotten a reputation as a bad-news people,
you people of Judah and Israel, but I'm coming to save
you. From now on, you're the good-news people.
Don't be afraid. Keep a firm grip on what I'm doing.*

ZECHARIAH 8:13 MSG

*A simple life in the Fear-of-God is better than
a rich life with a ton of headaches.*

PROVERBS 15:16 MSG

*Here is a simple, rule-of-thumb for behavior:
Ask yourself what you want people to do for you,
then grab the initiative and do it for them. Add up
God's Law and Prophets and this is what you get.*

MATTHEW 7:12 MSG

*He sent them off with these instructions:
"Don't think you need a lot of extra equipment for this.
You are the equipment. No special appeals for funds.
Keep it simple."*

MARK 6:8 MSG

THE LORD PRESERVES THE SIMPLE;
I WAS BROUGHT LOW,
AND HE SAVED ME.

PSALM 116:6 NASB